50 No Rules Just Flavor Recipes

By: Kelly Johnson

Table of Contents

- Spicy Honey Garlic Wings
- Kimchi Grilled Cheese
- Mango Habanero Tacos
- Cajun Shrimp Pasta
- Garlic Butter Smash Potatoes
- Sriracha Mac and Cheese
- Chimichurri Steak Bites
- Buffalo Cauliflower Wraps
- Pineapple Jerk Chicken
- Miso Ramen with Jammy Eggs
- Korean BBQ Beef Sliders
- Chili Lime Elote (Street Corn)
- Teriyaki Glazed Salmon
- Gochujang Fried Rice
- Honey Mustard Pretzel Chicken
- Dirty South BBQ Nachos
- Coconut Curry Meatballs

- Jalapeño Popper Quesadillas
- Spicy Peanut Noodles
- Bourbon Maple Glazed Ribs
- Bacon-Wrapped Avocado Fries
- Thai Basil Chicken
- Balsamic Roasted Brussels
- Black Garlic Alfredo
- Smoky Chipotle Tofu Bowls
- Hot Honey Fried Chicken Sandwich
- Firecracker Shrimp Tacos
- Nashville Hot Mac
- Truffle Parmesan Fries
- Roasted Red Pepper Hummus Flatbread
- Sweet Chili Chicken Stir Fry
- Lemon Dill Crispy Potatoes
- Spicy Mango Slaw Burgers
- Harissa Roasted Veggie Bowl
- Blackened Fish Tacos
- Maple Sriracha Brussels Skewers

- Garlic Parm Chicken Tenders
- Crunchy Thai Peanut Salad
- Cucumber Chili Soba Noodles
- Cajun Dirty Rice
- Sticky Sesame Cauliflower
- Tangy Tamarind Chicken Wings
- Zesty Lime Butter Corn
- Sweet Soy Glazed Meatballs
- Roasted Jalapeño Lime Dip
- Butter Chicken Nachos
- Street-Style Breakfast Tacos
- Avocado Salsa Chicken Bake
- Creamy Chipotle Penne
- Fried Pickle Grilled Cheese

Spicy Honey Garlic Wings

Ingredients:

- 2 lbs chicken wings
- 1/2 cup honey
- 1/4 cup soy sauce
- 5 garlic cloves, minced
- 2 tbsp sriracha (or to taste)
- 1 tbsp rice vinegar
- 1 tbsp olive oil
- Salt and pepper

Instructions:

1. Preheat oven to 400°F (200°C). Line a baking sheet with foil and a wire rack.
2. Season wings with salt and pepper. Place them on the rack and bake for 40–45 minutes, flipping halfway.
3. In a saucepan, heat oil over medium. Add garlic and sauté until fragrant.
4. Add honey, soy sauce, sriracha, and vinegar. Simmer for 3–5 minutes until slightly thickened.
5. Toss cooked wings in the sauce or brush it on and broil for 3–5 minutes for a sticky finish.

Kimchi Grilled Cheese

Ingredients:

- 2 slices of sourdough or bread of choice
- 1/2 cup shredded cheddar (or mozzarella mix)
- 1/3 cup chopped kimchi
- 1 tbsp butter

Instructions:

1. Butter one side of each bread slice.
2. Place one slice (butter side down) on a skillet, add cheese, then kimchi, and top with the other slice (butter side up).
3. Grill on medium heat until golden brown and the cheese is melted, about 3–4 minutes per side.

Mango Habanero Tacos

Ingredients:

- 1 lb chicken or shrimp
- 1 ripe mango, diced
- 1 habanero, finely chopped (remove seeds for less heat)
- 1/4 cup red onion, finely chopped
- 1/2 lime, juiced
- 1 tbsp olive oil
- Salt to taste
- Small tortillas
- Cilantro for garnish

Instructions:

1. In a bowl, mix mango, habanero, onion, lime juice, and a pinch of salt. Let it chill.
2. Cook seasoned chicken or shrimp in olive oil until done.
3. Warm tortillas, add protein, top with mango salsa, and garnish with cilantro.

Cajun Shrimp Pasta

Ingredients:

- 1 lb shrimp, peeled and deveined
- 8 oz fettuccine or pasta of choice
- 1 tbsp Cajun seasoning
- 1 cup heavy cream
- 1/2 cup grated Parmesan
- 2 tbsp butter
- 2 garlic cloves, minced
- Salt and pepper

Instructions:

1. Cook pasta according to package.
2. Season shrimp with Cajun seasoning. In a skillet, melt butter and cook shrimp 2–3 minutes per side. Remove.
3. In the same pan, sauté garlic, then pour in cream. Simmer and stir in Parmesan.
4. Add pasta and shrimp back to the skillet, toss to coat, and serve hot.

Garlic Butter Smash Potatoes

Ingredients:

- 1.5 lbs baby potatoes
- 3 tbsp butter, melted
- 3 garlic cloves, minced
- 1 tbsp olive oil
- Salt, pepper, fresh herbs (parsley or thyme)

Instructions:

1. Boil potatoes until fork tender, about 15–20 minutes.
2. Preheat oven to 425°F (220°C). Place boiled potatoes on a baking sheet and gently smash with a glass.
3. Mix butter, garlic, and oil. Brush over potatoes. Season with salt and pepper.
4. Roast for 25–30 minutes until crispy. Sprinkle with herbs before serving.

Sriracha Mac and Cheese

Ingredients:

- 8 oz elbow macaroni
- 2 tbsp butter
- 2 tbsp flour
- 2 cups milk
- 2 cups shredded cheddar
- 2 tbsp sriracha (adjust to taste)
- Salt to taste

Instructions:

1. Cook pasta and drain.
2. In a saucepan, melt butter and stir in flour to make a roux.
3. Slowly whisk in milk until smooth. Cook until thickened.
4. Add cheese and stir until melted. Mix in sriracha.
5. Combine with cooked pasta and serve warm.

Chimichurri Steak Bites

Ingredients:

- 1 lb sirloin steak, cut into bite-size cubes
- Salt and pepper
- 1 tbsp olive oil

For Chimichurri:

- 1/2 cup parsley, finely chopped
- 3 garlic cloves, minced
- 2 tbsp red wine vinegar
- 1/2 tsp red pepper flakes
- 1/4 cup olive oil
- Salt to taste

Instructions:

1. Mix chimichurri ingredients in a bowl. Let it sit for 10+ minutes.
2. Season steak bites with salt and pepper.
3. Heat olive oil in a skillet and sear steak bites 2–3 minutes per side.
4. Drizzle with chimichurri and serve immediately.

Buffalo Cauliflower Wraps

Ingredients:

- 1 small head cauliflower, cut into florets
- 1/2 cup flour
- 1/2 cup water
- 1/2 tsp garlic powder
- 1/2 cup buffalo sauce
- Tortillas or lettuce wraps
- Optional: ranch dressing, shredded lettuce, carrots

Instructions:

1. Preheat oven to 425°F (220°C).
2. Mix flour, water, and garlic powder into a batter. Coat cauliflower and place on a lined baking sheet.
3. Bake for 20 minutes. Remove and toss with buffalo sauce, then return to oven for 10 more minutes.
4. Load into wraps with toppings and drizzle with ranch.

Pineapple Jerk Chicken

Ingredients:

- 1.5 lbs chicken thighs or breasts
- 1 cup pineapple juice
- 2 tbsp soy sauce
- 1 tbsp brown sugar
- 1 tbsp jerk seasoning
- 1/2 tsp allspice
- 1/2 tsp thyme
- 1 tbsp olive oil
- Optional: pineapple chunks

Instructions:

1. Mix pineapple juice, soy sauce, sugar, jerk seasoning, allspice, thyme, and oil.
2. Marinate chicken for at least 1 hour (overnight best).
3. Grill or pan-sear chicken until cooked through and caramelized.
4. Serve with rice, grilled pineapple, or veggies.

Miso Ramen with Jammy Eggs

Ingredients:

- 2 packs ramen noodles (discard seasoning)
- 1 tbsp sesame oil
- 1 tbsp white miso paste
- 1 tbsp soy sauce
- 1 tsp grated ginger
- 2 garlic cloves, minced
- 4 cups chicken or vegetable broth
- 2 eggs
- Toppings: green onions, nori, mushrooms, corn, chili oil

Instructions:

1. Boil eggs for 6–7 minutes for jammy centers. Transfer to ice water, peel gently.
2. In a pot, heat sesame oil. Add garlic and ginger, cook until fragrant. Stir in miso paste and soy sauce.
3. Pour in broth, bring to a simmer.
4. Cook ramen noodles in the broth.
5. Serve noodles in bowls, top with halved eggs and desired toppings.

Korean BBQ Beef Sliders

Ingredients:

- 1 lb ground beef or thinly sliced short rib
- 2 tbsp soy sauce
- 1 tbsp brown sugar
- 1 tbsp gochujang (Korean chili paste)
- 1 tsp sesame oil
- 1 garlic clove, minced
- Slider buns
- Kimchi and sliced cucumber for topping

Instructions:

1. In a bowl, combine beef, soy sauce, sugar, gochujang, sesame oil, and garlic. Let marinate 20+ minutes.
2. Grill or pan-fry beef until cooked through.
3. Toast slider buns.
4. Assemble with beef, kimchi, and cucumber slices.

Chili Lime Elote (Street Corn)

Ingredients:

- 4 ears corn, grilled or boiled
- 1/4 cup mayonnaise
- 1/4 cup sour cream
- 1/2 cup cotija cheese, crumbled
- 1 tbsp lime juice
- 1 tsp chili powder
- Cilantro and lime wedges

Instructions:

1. Mix mayo, sour cream, lime juice, and chili powder.
2. Brush mixture over hot corn.
3. Sprinkle generously with cotija and garnish with cilantro.
4. Serve with lime wedges.

Teriyaki Glazed Salmon

Ingredients:

- 4 salmon fillets
- 1/3 cup soy sauce
- 1/4 cup honey or brown sugar
- 1 tbsp rice vinegar
- 2 garlic cloves, minced
- 1 tsp ginger, grated
- 1 tsp cornstarch + 1 tbsp water

Instructions:

1. In a saucepan, combine soy sauce, honey, vinegar, garlic, and ginger. Simmer.
2. Mix cornstarch slurry and add to sauce. Stir until thickened.
3. Pan-sear salmon skin-side down for 3–4 minutes, flip and brush with sauce.
4. Cook until just done, brush with more glaze before serving.

Gochujang Fried Rice

Ingredients:

- 2 cups cooked rice (cold works best)
- 2 eggs
- 1/2 onion, diced
- 2 green onions, sliced
- 1 tbsp gochujang
- 1 tbsp soy sauce
- 1 tsp sesame oil
- Optional: diced spam, bacon, or tofu

Instructions:

1. Scramble eggs in oil, set aside.
2. In the same pan, sauté onion (and protein if using).
3. Add rice, break it apart, then stir in gochujang, soy sauce, and sesame oil.
4. Mix in cooked egg and green onions.

Honey Mustard Pretzel Chicken

Ingredients:

- 1 lb chicken tenders or breast strips
- 1 cup crushed pretzels
- 1/2 cup flour
- 2 eggs, beaten
- 1/4 cup honey
- 1/4 cup Dijon mustard

Instructions:

1. Preheat oven to 400°F (200°C).
2. Dredge chicken in flour, dip in egg, then coat in crushed pretzels.
3. Place on baking sheet, bake for 20–25 minutes or until golden and cooked through.
4. Mix honey and mustard, serve as dipping sauce.

Dirty South BBQ Nachos

Ingredients:

- Tortilla chips
- 1 cup pulled pork or shredded chicken
- 1/2 cup BBQ sauce
- 1 cup shredded cheese (cheddar or blend)
- Pickled jalapeños
- Green onions
- Sour cream or ranch drizzle

Instructions:

1. Preheat oven to 375°F (190°C).
2. Layer chips on a baking tray, top with BBQ meat and cheese.
3. Bake until cheese melts, about 10 minutes.
4. Top with jalapeños, green onions, and drizzle with sour cream or ranch.

Coconut Curry Meatballs

Ingredients:

- 1 lb ground chicken or turkey
- 1 egg
- 1/4 cup breadcrumbs
- 1 garlic clove, minced
- 1 tsp ginger, grated
- 1 can coconut milk
- 2 tbsp red curry paste
- 1 tbsp fish sauce
- Lime and cilantro

Instructions:

1. Mix meat, egg, breadcrumbs, garlic, and ginger. Form into small meatballs.
2. Brown meatballs in a skillet, then remove.
3. In same pan, combine curry paste and coconut milk. Stir in fish sauce.
4. Return meatballs to pan and simmer until cooked through. Garnish with lime and cilantro.

Jalapeño Popper Quesadillas
Ingredients:

- 4 flour tortillas
- 1/2 cup cream cheese, softened
- 1 cup shredded cheddar
- 2–3 jalapeños, sliced or chopped
- 4 slices cooked bacon, crumbled (optional)
- Butter for toasting

Instructions:

1. Spread cream cheese on one side of each tortilla.
2. Add cheddar, jalapeños, and bacon. Fold tortillas in half.
3. Cook in a buttered skillet until golden and melty, 2–3 minutes per side.
4. Slice and serve with salsa or sour cream.

Spicy Peanut Noodles

Ingredients:

- 8 oz noodles (ramen, soba, or spaghetti)
- 1/4 cup peanut butter
- 2 tbsp soy sauce
- 1 tbsp rice vinegar
- 1 tbsp sriracha
- 1 tsp sesame oil
- 1 tsp honey
- 1 garlic clove, minced
- Chopped green onions, sesame seeds, crushed peanuts

Instructions:

1. Cook noodles according to package. Drain and rinse with cold water.
2. In a bowl, whisk peanut butter, soy sauce, vinegar, sriracha, sesame oil, honey, and garlic.
3. Toss noodles in sauce until coated.
4. Top with green onions, peanuts, and sesame seeds.

Bourbon Maple Glazed Ribs

Ingredients:

- 2 racks pork ribs
- Salt, pepper, paprika
- 1/4 cup bourbon
- 1/4 cup maple syrup
- 2 tbsp soy sauce
- 1 tbsp Dijon mustard
- 2 garlic cloves, minced

Instructions:

1. Rub ribs with salt, pepper, and paprika. Wrap in foil.
2. Bake at 300°F (150°C) for 2.5–3 hours.
3. Simmer bourbon, maple, soy sauce, mustard, and garlic into a glaze.
4. Unwrap ribs, brush with glaze, and broil until sticky and caramelized.

Bacon-Wrapped Avocado Fries

Ingredients:

- 2 ripe avocados, sliced into wedges
- 10–12 strips of bacon
- Optional: chili powder or black pepper

Instructions:

1. Wrap each avocado wedge in bacon.
2. Secure with toothpicks if needed.
3. Bake at 425°F (220°C) for 12–15 minutes, turning once, until crispy.
4. Serve with ranch or chipotle mayo.

Thai Basil Chicken (Pad Krapow Gai)

Ingredients:

- 1 lb ground chicken
- 4 garlic cloves, minced
- 2 Thai chilies, finely chopped (or to taste)
- 2 tbsp soy sauce
- 1 tbsp oyster sauce
- 1 tsp fish sauce
- 1 tsp sugar
- 1/2 cup fresh Thai basil leaves

Instructions:

1. Sauté garlic and chilies in oil until fragrant.
2. Add chicken, cook until browned.
3. Stir in sauces and sugar. Cook 2–3 more minutes.
4. Fold in Thai basil until wilted.
5. Serve with rice and a fried egg on top.

Balsamic Roasted Brussels

Ingredients:

- 1 lb Brussels sprouts, halved
- 2 tbsp olive oil
- Salt and pepper
- 2 tbsp balsamic glaze or reduction

Instructions:

1. Toss Brussels with oil, salt, and pepper.
2. Roast at 425°F (220°C) for 20–25 minutes until crispy.
3. Drizzle with balsamic glaze before serving.

Black Garlic Alfredo

Ingredients:

- 8 oz fettuccine or pasta of choice
- 4 cloves black garlic, mashed
- 2 tbsp butter
- 1 cup heavy cream
- 1/2 cup grated Parmesan
- Salt, pepper to taste

Instructions:

1. Cook pasta, reserve some water.
2. Melt butter in pan, add mashed black garlic.
3. Stir in cream, simmer. Add Parmesan, stir until smooth.
4. Toss with pasta, add pasta water to loosen if needed.
5. Serve hot, top with more Parmesan.

Smoky Chipotle Tofu Bowls

Ingredients:

- 1 block extra firm tofu, pressed and cubed
- 2 tbsp chipotle in adobo, chopped
- 1 tbsp olive oil
- 1 tsp smoked paprika
- Cooked rice or quinoa
- Avocado, corn, lime, black beans, cilantro for topping

Instructions:

1. Toss tofu with chipotle, oil, and paprika.
2. Bake at 400°F (200°C) for 25–30 minutes until crisp.
3. Build bowls with grains, tofu, and toppings.
4. Finish with lime juice and cilantro.

Hot Honey Fried Chicken Sandwich
Ingredients:

- 2 chicken breasts, butterflied
- 1 cup buttermilk
- 1 cup flour + 1 tsp paprika
- Oil for frying
- 2 tbsp honey + 1 tsp hot sauce
- Brioche buns, pickles, slaw (optional)

Instructions:

1. Marinate chicken in buttermilk 1 hour or overnight.
2. Dredge in seasoned flour.
3. Fry at 350°F (175°C) until golden and cooked through.
4. Mix honey and hot sauce, drizzle on chicken.
5. Serve on buns with pickles and slaw.

Firecracker Shrimp Tacos

Ingredients:

- 1 lb shrimp, peeled
- 1/4 cup mayo
- 1 tbsp sriracha
- 1 tbsp honey
- 1 tsp soy sauce
- Tortillas, slaw mix, lime

Instructions:

1. Mix sauce ingredients (mayo, sriracha, honey, soy).
2. Sauté shrimp in a hot pan until pink. Toss with sauce.
3. Serve in warm tortillas with slaw and lime wedges.

Nashville Hot Mac

Ingredients:

- 8 oz elbow macaroni
- 2 tbsp butter
- 2 tbsp flour
- 2 cups milk
- 2 cups shredded cheese (cheddar or blend)
- 1 tsp cayenne
- 1 tsp paprika
- 1/2 tsp garlic powder
- 1/2 tsp hot sauce
- Optional: breadcrumbs toasted in butter

Instructions:

1. Cook pasta.
2. Make roux with butter and flour. Slowly add milk, stir until thick.
3. Add cheese and spices, mix until smooth.
4. Stir in pasta and hot sauce.
5. Top with toasted breadcrumbs if desired.

Truffle Parmesan Fries

Ingredients:

- 3 large russet potatoes, cut into fries
- 2 tbsp olive oil
- 1–2 tsp truffle oil (to taste)
- Salt, black pepper
- 1/4 cup grated Parmesan
- Chopped parsley (optional)

Instructions:

1. Soak fries in cold water 30 min, then dry well.
2. Toss with olive oil, salt, pepper.
3. Bake at 425°F (220°C) for 30–35 min, flipping halfway.
4. Drizzle with truffle oil, sprinkle with Parmesan and parsley.

Roasted Red Pepper Hummus Flatbread

Ingredients:

- Flatbreads or naan
- 1 cup roasted red pepper hummus
- Cherry tomatoes, sliced cucumbers, olives, arugula
- Crumbled feta
- Olive oil, lemon juice

Instructions:

1. Warm flatbread in oven or skillet.
2. Spread hummus generously.
3. Top with veggies, feta, a drizzle of olive oil, and a squeeze of lemon.

Sweet Chili Chicken Stir Fry

Ingredients:

- 1 lb chicken breast, thinly sliced
- 2 cups mixed stir-fry veggies
- 1/3 cup sweet chili sauce
- 1 tbsp soy sauce
- 1 tsp sesame oil
- Cooked jasmine rice

Instructions:

1. Sear chicken in a hot pan until golden. Remove.
2. Stir-fry veggies until tender.
3. Add chicken back in, pour in sauces.
4. Toss to coat, serve over rice.

Lemon Dill Crispy Potatoes

Ingredients:

- 1.5 lb baby potatoes
- 2 tbsp olive oil
- Juice of 1 lemon
- 1 tsp dried dill (or fresh)
- Salt, pepper

Instructions:

1. Boil potatoes until tender. Drain and smash slightly.
2. Roast at 425°F (220°C) with oil, salt, pepper for 25 min.
3. Toss with lemon juice and dill while hot.

Spicy Mango Slaw Burgers

Ingredients:

- 1 lb ground beef or plant-based patties
- Burger buns
- 1 cup shredded cabbage
- 1/2 cup mango, diced
- 1 tbsp lime juice
- 1 tsp sriracha
- Mayo

Instructions:

1. Mix slaw ingredients: cabbage, mango, lime, sriracha.
2. Cook patties to desired doneness.
3. Toast buns, layer with mayo, burger, slaw.

Harissa Roasted Veggie Bowl

Ingredients:

- 2 cups chopped mixed vegetables (cauliflower, carrots, zucchini, etc.)
- 2 tbsp harissa paste
- 1 tbsp olive oil
- Cooked couscous or quinoa
- Yogurt or tahini for drizzle

Instructions:

1. Toss veggies with harissa and olive oil.
2. Roast at 400°F (200°C) for 25–30 minutes.
3. Serve over grains, drizzle with yogurt or tahini.

Blackened Fish Tacos

Ingredients:

- 1 lb white fish (tilapia, cod)
- 1 tbsp blackening seasoning
- Corn tortillas
- Slaw or shredded lettuce
- Lime wedges, crema or sour cream

Instructions:

1. Rub fish with seasoning, cook in skillet 3–4 min per side.
2. Warm tortillas, fill with fish and slaw.
3. Squeeze lime over top, add crema.

Maple Sriracha Brussels Skewers

Ingredients:

- 1 lb Brussels sprouts, halved
- 2 tbsp maple syrup
- 1 tbsp sriracha
- 1 tbsp olive oil
- Salt

Instructions:

1. Toss Brussels with maple, sriracha, oil, and salt.
2. Skewer and roast at 400°F (200°C) for 25–30 minutes.
3. Serve hot with extra sauce on the side.

Garlic Parm Chicken Tenders
 Ingredients:

- 1 lb chicken tenders
- 1/2 cup breadcrumbs
- 1/4 cup grated Parmesan
- 1 tsp garlic powder
- 1 egg, beaten

Instructions:

1. Mix breadcrumbs, Parmesan, and garlic powder.
2. Dip chicken in egg, then breadcrumb mixture.
3. Bake at 400°F (200°C) for 20–25 min or air fry until golden.

Crunchy Thai Peanut Salad

Ingredients:

- 2 cups shredded cabbage
- 1 carrot, julienned
- 1/2 red bell pepper, thinly sliced
- 1/4 cup chopped peanuts
- Chopped cilantro, green onions
- **Dressing:** 2 tbsp peanut butter, 1 tbsp lime juice, 1 tbsp soy sauce, 1 tsp honey, 1 tsp sesame oil

Instructions:

1. Whisk dressing ingredients until smooth.
2. Toss all salad components with dressing.
3. Top with peanuts and fresh herbs.

Cucumber Chili Soba Noodles

Ingredients:

- 8 oz soba noodles
- 1 cucumber, julienned
- 1 tbsp chili crisp or chili oil
- 2 tbsp soy sauce
- 1 tbsp rice vinegar
- 1 tsp sesame oil
- Sesame seeds, green onions

Instructions:

1. Cook soba noodles, rinse with cold water.
2. Toss with cucumber, chili oil, soy sauce, vinegar, and sesame oil.
3. Top with sesame seeds and green onions.

Cajun Dirty Rice

Ingredients:

- 1 cup long-grain rice
- 1/2 lb ground sausage
- 1/2 onion, diced
- 1 celery stalk, diced
- 1/2 bell pepper, diced
- 2 tsp Cajun seasoning
- 2 cups chicken broth

Instructions:

1. Brown sausage, then add onion, celery, and bell pepper. Cook until soft.
2. Stir in Cajun seasoning, rice, and broth.
3. Simmer covered for 18–20 minutes until rice is cooked.

Sticky Sesame Cauliflower

Ingredients:

- 1 head cauliflower, cut into florets
- 1/2 cup flour
- 1/2 cup water
- 1/2 cup panko
- **Sauce:** 1/4 cup soy sauce, 2 tbsp honey, 1 tbsp rice vinegar, 1 tsp sesame oil, 1 tsp cornstarch
- Sesame seeds, green onions

Instructions:

1. Dip cauliflower in flour-water mix, then panko.
2. Bake at 425°F (220°C) for 25 min.
3. Simmer sauce until thick, toss with roasted cauliflower.
4. Garnish with sesame seeds and green onions.

Tangy Tamarind Chicken Wings
Ingredients:

- 2 lbs chicken wings
- 2 tbsp tamarind paste
- 1 tbsp soy sauce
- 1 tbsp brown sugar
- 1 tsp garlic powder
- 1 tsp chili flakes

Instructions:

1. Mix tamarind, soy, sugar, garlic powder, and chili flakes.
2. Marinate wings at least 1 hour.
3. Bake at 400°F (200°C) for 40–45 minutes, basting halfway.
4. Broil last 2 minutes for crispy finish.

Zesty Lime Butter Corn

Ingredients:

- 4 ears corn, husked
- 2 tbsp butter
- Zest and juice of 1 lime
- Salt, chili powder (optional)

Instructions:

1. Grill or boil corn until tender.
2. Melt butter with lime juice and zest.
3. Brush over hot corn and sprinkle with salt or chili powder.

Sweet Soy Glazed Meatballs

Ingredients:

- 1 lb ground beef or turkey
- 1 egg
- 1/4 cup breadcrumbs
- 1 garlic clove, minced
- **Glaze:** 1/4 cup soy sauce, 2 tbsp brown sugar, 1 tbsp rice vinegar, 1 tsp cornstarch

Instructions:

1. Mix meatball ingredients, form small balls.
2. Bake or pan-fry until cooked through.
3. Simmer glaze ingredients until thick.
4. Toss meatballs in glaze and serve.

Roasted Jalapeño Lime Dip

Ingredients:

- 2 jalapeños, roasted and peeled
- 1/2 cup sour cream
- 1/4 cup cream cheese
- Juice of 1 lime
- 1 garlic clove
- Salt, pepper

Instructions:

1. Blend all ingredients until smooth.
2. Chill before serving for best flavor.
3. Serve with chips, veggies, or spread on sandwiches.

Butter Chicken Nachos

Ingredients:

- Tortilla chips
- 1 cup cooked butter chicken (shredded)
- 1/2 cup shredded cheese
- Chopped red onion, jalapeños, cilantro
- Yogurt or sour cream

Instructions:

1. Layer chips with butter chicken and cheese.
2. Bake at 375°F (190°C) for 8–10 minutes.
3. Top with onions, jalapeños, cilantro, and a dollop of yogurt.

Street-Style Breakfast Tacos
 Ingredients:

- 4 small flour or corn tortillas
- 4 scrambled eggs
- 1/4 cup cooked breakfast sausage or chorizo
- Diced onion, fresh cilantro
- Salsa, hot sauce, lime wedges

Instructions:

1. Warm tortillas on skillet.
2. Fill with eggs, sausage, onions, cilantro.
3. Finish with salsa and lime.

Avocado Salsa Chicken Bake

Ingredients:

- 2 chicken breasts
- 1 avocado, diced
- 1/3 cup salsa
- 1/4 cup shredded cheese
- Salt, pepper, cumin

Instructions:

1. Season chicken with salt, pepper, cumin.
2. Bake at 375°F (190°C) for 20 minutes.
3. Top with avocado, salsa, cheese.
4. Bake 5–10 more minutes until melted and bubbly.

Creamy Chipotle Penne

Ingredients:

- 8 oz penne pasta
- 1 tbsp butter
- 1 garlic clove, minced
- 1 chipotle pepper in adobo, minced
- 1/2 cup heavy cream
- 1/4 cup grated Parmesan

Instructions:

1. Cook pasta, set aside.
2. In a skillet, melt butter and sauté garlic and chipotle.
3. Stir in cream and Parmesan, simmer until thick.
4. Toss pasta in sauce and serve hot.

Fried Pickle Grilled Cheese

Ingredients:

- 2 slices sourdough bread
- 4–5 pickle slices
- 2 slices cheddar or American cheese
- 1 tbsp mayo or butter
- Optional: a dash of hot sauce

Instructions:

1. Layer pickles and cheese between bread slices.
2. Spread mayo or butter on the outside.
3. Grill on skillet until golden brown and melty.
4. Slice and serve with extra pickles or dipping sauce.